DAILY DEVOTIONS

FOR GEN Z

Jace Hunter

Tea On Devotional Slaps

Aight, so here's the tea on why a Gen Z devotional slaps: it's like having a life coach in your pocket that speaks your language. No cap, it's tailored for the way we scroll, snap, and text, but it's all about leveling up the soul, you feel me?

This devotional isn't just some dusty old scripture—it's fresh, it's now, it's the spiritual hype you need to keep your head and your heart in the game. It's 100% about connecting those ancient truths to our modern-day hustles. It's like that bridge between Sunday school and your everyday school, work, and social life.

Each day, you get this bite-sized piece of heaven that fits right between your TikToks and your tweets. It's low-key enough to not overwhelm but deep enough to make you think. It's about getting that daily dose of positivity, purpose, and perspective.

So, whether you're dealing with drama, chasing dreams, or just trying to stay woke, a Gen Z devotional is like your spiritual battery pack, keeping you charged, centered, and ready to face the world's static. It's not just about faith; it's about finding your way. And that's the real glow-up. 🔋🔌🙌

week 1

Day 1

No Cap, God's Love Is Lit

Verse of the Day: "God is love. Whoever lives in love lives in God, and God in them." - 1 John 4:16b (NIV)

Devotional:

Yo, peeps! Ever felt like love stories are just fairy tales? But here's the real tea: God's love is the ultimate no cap. It's not just a mood; it's the whole vibe. His love is more lit than your fav TikTok dance challenge.

Prayer:

Ayy, God, help me feel that high-key love You got for me. No flex, I want to spread that love like it's going viral. Amen.

Action:

Today, show some love to your squad. Share a compliment, send a meme that'll make them laugh, or just check in. Spread that God-type love.

Day 2

Trust the process, Not the stress

Verse of the Day: "Trust in the Lord with all your heart and lean not on your own understanding." - Proverbs 3:5 (NIV)

Devotional:

Fam, we all get shook when things don't go as planned. But here's the thing: God's asking us to trust the process, not the stress. When your brain is buffering, remember God's connection never lags.

Prayer:

Yo, it's ya boi/girl (your name). Sometimes I'm lowkey stressed about the future. Slide me some of that peace and trust, will ya? Bet.

Action:

When you're feeling anxious today, take a minute to just breathe. Remember, God's got the ultimate game plan.

Day 3

Swipe Right on Kindness

Verse of the Day: "Be kind and compassionate to one another, forgiving each other, just as in Christ God forgave you." - Ephesians 4:32 (NIV)

Devotional:

We all know the drill: Swipe right if you're into it, left if you're not. But when it comes to kindness, it's a hard right swipe every time. Let's be those people who double-tap on compassion IRL.

Prayer:

Hey, Big Guy, sometimes it's hard to hit that like button on people who test my patience. Download some of your kindness into my heart's app, yeah? Thanks, fam.

Action:

Find someone who needs a boost and drop a kind comment or a small act of kindness their way. Make kindness go viral in your community.

Day 4

Ghost fear, Flex faith

Verse of the Day: "For God has not given us a spirit of fear, but of power and of love and of a sound mind." - 2 Timothy 1:7 (NKJV)

Devotional:

Ghouls and ghosts are for Halloween, not your headspace. If fear's tryna haunt you, it's time to ghost it and flex that faith muscle. Remember, God's spirit is like the ultimate gym trainer for your soul.

Prayer:

Ayy, Coach in the heavens, fear's tryna bench me. Hook me

up with your power-up so I can yeet this anxiety and boss up.

You feel me?

Action:

Whenever fear tries to slide into your DMs today, hit it with a

faith block. Remind yourself who's really got your back.

Day 5

Stay Hydrated with the Word

Verse of the Day: "But whoever drinks the water I give them will never thirst." - John 4:14a (NIV)

Devotional:

Just like you keep sipping that H2O to stay hydrated, sip on the Word to keep your soul quenched. God's truth is like the ultimate thirst quencher – it keeps you from getting spiritually parched.

Prayer:

Lord, sometimes I'm just out here in the desert of life feeling

all kinds of thirsty. Pour out that living water on me. I'm here

with my cup ready. Fill 'er up!

Action:

Dive into a passage from the Bible today. Let it refresh you

like a cold drink on a hot day.

Day 6

Send Negativity to Voicemail

Verse of the Day: "Do not be overcome by evil, but overcome evil with good." - Romans 12:21 (NIV)

Devotional:

Yo, peeps, today's the day we hit 'ignore' on those bad vibes. Keep your mental on airplane mode when drama's trying to land. Let's keep our inner peace on lock and our energy 100. No cap, just good vibes only.

Prayer:

Aight, Big Boss in the sky, hook me up with that mental 'Do Not Disturb'. When the negativity hits, help me press decline. Only got space for love and laughs in my soul's contacts. Amen.

Action:

Catch a whiff of that toxic talk? Slide it to voicemail. Hit 'em with kindness or just keep it moving. Your day's playlist is all love, no skips. Keep your spirit's battery charged to full.

Day 7

Vibing High on God's Frequency

Verse of the day: "Finally, brothers and sisters, whatever is true, whatever is noble, whatever is right, whatever is pure, whatever is lovely, whatever is admirable—if anything is excellent or praiseworthy—think about such things."- Philippians 4:8(NJV)

Devotional:

Alright, Day 7, let's get this bread, fam. Today, we're tuning into God's frequency—pure, uncut, and straight fire. Stack your thoughts with that premium content—stuff that's true, noble, right, and pure. Let your mind marinate in the excellence of the Most High and keep your spiritual Wi-Fi looking for His signals.

Prayer:

Lord, let my thoughts be like the sickest playlist, curated by You. When the low-fi static of life tries to mess with my signal, remind me to hit up the tracks You've dropped—those Philippians 4:8 vibes. Keep my spirit streaming Your divine beats, 24/7. Amen.

Action:

Today, challenge yourself to peep only the good stuff. Slide into someone's DMs with a hype message, drop a fire emoji on a friend's wholesome post, and ghost any threads of negativity. Keep your headspace as clean as a fresh pair of

kicks. And remember, what you vibe, you become—so keep it

righteous, keep it tight.

week 2

Day 1

God's plan is the ultimate Glow-up

Verse of the Day: Jeremiah 29:11 - "For I know the plans I have for you," declares the Lord, "plans to prosper you and not to harm you, plans to give you hope and a future."

Devotional:

Y'all, we all have those days when we're feelin' kinda basic, but remember God's got a plan that's more fire than our fave influencer's feed. He's got that blueprint for your glow-up, no clickbait.

Prayer:

Yo, it's your kiddo on the line. Just need that reminder that Your plan is more lit than any glow-up challenge. Keep me on that righteous path, no cap.

Action:

Today, when you're feeling like a flop, remember you're actually a work in progress. Post a note or set a reminder with Jer 29:11 to keep that front and center.

Day 2

Squad Goals with the Almighty

Verse of the Day: Ecclesiastes 4:12 - "Though one may be overpowered, two can defend themselves. A cord of three strands is not quickly broken."

Devotional:

Listen up, fam. Your squad is key, right? But imagine rolling with the Almighty in your crew. That's the ultimate squad goal. With God, you're rolling three deep, and that's the kind of support that doesn't ghost.

Prayer:

God, thanks for being part of my squad and for the real ones You've blessed me with. Help us to be like that three-strand cord – tight, strong, and not easily snapped.

Action:

Hit up your friends today with some encouragement. Remind them they're part of your God squad and you're stronger together.

Day 3

Throwing Shade? Nah, We Project

Light

Verse of the Day: Matthew 5:16 - "In the same way, let your light shine before others, that they may see your good deeds and glorify your Father in heaven."

Devotional:

We all know someone who's all about throwing shade, but we're called to be about that light life. Flip the script and project those good vibes and deeds that spotlight the Big G upstairs.

Prayer:

Hey, Chief Light Officer, show me how to flip on that high beam and light up the room with Your vibe, not mine. Help me reflect Your light, not throw shade.

Action:

Do something low key kind for someone today and keep it hush. It's not for the 'Gram; it's for the Man upstairs.

Day 4

Keep It Real, Keep It Righteous

Verse of the Day: Proverbs 21:3 - "To do what is right and just is more acceptable to the Lord than sacrifice."

Devotional:

It's easy to get caught up in the show, doing stuff for the likes. But keeping it 100 with what's right and just? That's the content God double-taps.

Prayer:

God, you know I wanna keep it real for You. Guide me to do what's right, not just what gets me hype. Let me live for that 'Well done, good and faithful servant,' not just the dopamine hits.

Action:

Before you make moves today, ask yourself if it's for the clout or for what's right. Choose the righteous route.

Day 5

Don't Let the world Make You Salty

Verse of the Day: James 1:19-20 - "Everyone should be quick to listen, slow to speak and slow to become angry, because human anger does not produce the righteousness that God desires."

Devotional:

The world's always trying to make us salty, but that ain't the flavor God's after. He wants us to season our words with grace, not clap back with that high sodium content.

Prayer:

Lord, it's a salty world, and sometimes I wanna sprinkle that

back. Help me keep my cool and not be a salty snack.

Action:

Today, when you're on the brink of snapping back, take a

beat. Listen more, speak less, stay unseasoned.

Day 6

Slide into the DMs of the Downtrodden

Verse of the Day: 1 Thessalonians 5:11 - "Therefore encourage one another and build each other up, just as in fact you are doing."

Devotional:

We all love a good DM slide, especially when it's hyping us up. Slide into the DMs of someone who's feeling low with an encouraging word. Be that hype person.

Prayer:

Yo, God, you're the OG encourager. Help me to be a beast at lifting others up. Give me the words to send a message of hope to someone who needs it. Let me be a mirror of Your love, just doing my part to keep the squad strong.

Action:

Find someone in your circle, or even someone you haven't talked to in a hot minute, and send them a positive message. Could be a text, DM, or even a meme that says "I'm thinking of you!" Be intentional with your encouragement – it's like a direct deposit of joy to their soul.

Day 7

Self-Care Isn't Selfish, It's Scriptural

Verse of the Day: Mark 6:31 - "Then, because so many people were coming and going that they did not even have a chance to eat, he said to them, 'Come with me by yourselves to a quiet place and get some rest.'"

Devotional:

The hustle is real, but even Jesus knew when it was time to hit pause and recharge. Taking time for self-care isn't selfish; it's necessary. Don't burn out before you shine out.

Prayer:

Hey, Creator of Chill, help me to recognize when I need to power down and take care of myself. It's easy to get caught up in the grind, but I know that to do Your work, I need to be charged up. Bless my me-time so I can give more we-time.

Action:

Today, do something that recharges your batteries. Maybe it's a nap, a walk, some time with a book, or just vibing to your favorite music. Remember, taking care of you is part of taking care of His kingdom.

week 3

Day 1

G.O.D = Greatest of Dieties

Verse of the Day: Psalm 147:5 - "Great is our Lord and mighty in power; his understanding has no limit."

Devotional:

Let's kick it off with some real talk: the Big G is limitless, fam. His power? Off the charts. His wisdom? Unmatched. Dive into that infinity pool of divine swag today.

Prayer:

Yo, Big Homie in the Sky, thanks for being the ultimate. Teach me to tap into Your endless power and kick it with wisdom that only You can dish out. Keep it 💯.

Action:

Today, find a moment to just gaze at the sky or stars. Marvel at that divine artistry and remember who painted that vastness. Maybe snap a pic and share that wonder on your feed, sparking some cosmic contemplation among the peeps.

Day 2

Scriptural Sesh

Verse of the Day: 2 Timothy 3:16 - "All Scripture is God-breathed and is useful for teaching, rebuking, correcting, and training in righteousness."

Devotional:

Bible time isn't just for the 'Gram aesthetic. Those pages pack a punch, full of life hacks straight from Heaven's HQ. Get your daily dose of divine wisdom and let it amp up your soul game.

Prayer:

Aight, Author of Life, your Word is the ultimate clapback to life's mess. Help me digest those holy texts and flex some spiritual muscle. Amen!

Action:

Carve out a 10-minute power sesh with the Word. No distractions, just you and the scriptures. Find a verse that hits different and meditate on it. Maybe even make it your phone wallpaper to keep that wisdom front and center.

Day 3

Trust the Process

Verse of the Day: Proverbs 3:5-6 - "Trust in the Lord with all your heart and lean not on your own understanding; in all your ways submit to him, and he will make your paths straight."

Devotional:

Life's a wild ride, but trust in the Divine GPS to navigate the twisty roads. Your plans are dope, but His plans are doper. Let go and let God steer the way to straight-up blessings.

Prayer:

Yo, Navigator of the Universe, I'm buckling up for the ride You've got planned. I might not always get the route, but I trust Your directions are leading to someplace epic. Guide me, fam.

Action:

Today, take a situation that's got you stressing and offer it up. Say, "You got this, God," and focus on something you can control instead. Keep the faith and watch the path clear up.

Day 4

Love Hype

Verse of the Day: 1 John 4:19 - "We love because he first loved us."

Devotional:

We're all about that love life, 'cause that's the OG commandment. It started with the Man Upstairs, and now it's our turn to spread that good-good love like confetti.

Prayer:

Hey, Love Supreme, thanks for the feels and the real deal of Your heart. Help me to share that OG love today in ways that speak louder than any TikTok trend. Let's get this love party popping.

Action:

Shoot a message of love to three people today. Could be fam, friends, or that barista who nails your coffee order. Spread that affection like Wi-Fi, free and unconditional.

Day 5

Anxiety? Cancelled.

Verse of the Day: Philippians 4:6-7 - "Do not be anxious about anything, but in every situation, by prayer and petition, with thanksgiving, present your requests to God."

Devotional:

Anxiety's got no chill, but guess what? Prayer's got the power to hit that cancel button. Bring the Big G your worries and watch Him work His peace like a divine DJ.

Prayer:

Chief Comfort, my mind's a no-sleep zone with all these worries. I'm sliding these DMs to You 'cause I know You've got the peace hookup. Drop that serene beat in my heart.

Action:

When you feel the anxiety creeping, hit pause. Take five deep breaths. Each inhale, scoop up peace; each exhale, dump the stress. Then whisper a quick prayer to keep the vibes right.

Day 6

Faith FOMO? Nah.

Verse of the Day: Hebrews 11:1 - "Now faith is confidence in what we hope for and assurance about what we do not see."

Devotional:

Ever get FOMO scrolling through your feed seeing everyone's highlight reels? Flip the script. Get# 7-Day Devotional: Faith Vibes for Gen Z

Prayer:

Heavenly Creator, who vibes on a frequency higher than any signal,

Today, I'm scrollin' through the feed of my life, and sometimes I get hit with that FOMO—fear of missing out on what You have in store for me. I see the highlight reels of others, peep their blessings, and start to wonder about my own story.

In this hyper-connected world, help me to stay plugged into the main source—Your purpose and Your love. Teach me to trust the unseen, to have faith in the journey You've mapped out, even when the GPS seems to be glitching.

Lord, You're the ultimate influencer in my life. Help me to double-tap on the realness of Your promises and not just the hype of what I see. May my faith not be a trend that fades, but a constant connection to You.

As I swipe through the moments of my day, I ask for the courage to hit 'like' on the unfiltered reality of my path, the one You've crafted uniquely for me. Help me to remember that faith ain't just about the perfect, curated posts, but also about the candid, behind-the-scenes growth.

Bless me with the boldness to live out loud for You, to not just say I believe, but to show it in the way I snap back at life's challenges, in the DMs of encouragement I send, and in the stories I share that give You the glory.

I'm ready to drop the FOMO and pick up the JOMO—the joy of missing out on anything that isn't in Your plan. Guide me to focus on the blessings You've placed in my life and to influence others to get in on this joy too.

In Your holy handle's name, Amen. 🙌 📖 ✨

Action:

Yo, let's keep it real today and spread some of that good energy! It's all about making those moves that show your faith isn't just talk—it's big action energy. We're gonna slide into some generosity today and make it count.

Morning Vibes: Kick it off by counting your blessings. No cap, just straight-up thankfulness. Jot down three things you're totally vibing with and let that grateful mood set the tone for your day.

Afternoon Moves: Scope out someone who could use a boost. Maybe your squad mate is struggling or your fam could do with some extra love. Shoot them a text, drop a meme that says "I gotchu," or just lend an ear. It's all about those connections.

Evening Goals: Now's the time to flex that giving muscle. Whether it's throwing a few bucks to that GoFundMe that's been on your feed, helping out at the local food bank, or just being that surprise plug for someone's coffee—do something that makes someone else's day a little brighter.

When you hit the pillow tonight, reflect on that feel-good vibe you got from giving. It's like, when you focus on what you can give rather than what you're tryna get, everything flips and suddenly you're living in this abundance mindset.

It's a whole vibe, for real. Keep those positive actions rolling beyond today. Make it a habit, like checking your Insta stories or keeping your streaks alive. Keep it 100 and watch how that good karma circles back.

Stay lit, fam! 🌟🙌 #GiveBack #BlessedAndAGiver

Day 7

Level Up Your Faith Game

Verse of the Day: James 2:17 - "In the same way, faith by itself, if it is not accompanied by action, is dead."

Devotional:

We've been vibin' on this spiritual journey all week, and now it's time to level up. Faith ain't just about feeling blessed; it's about being a blessing. Put some sneakers on that faith and let it move you. Actions speak louder than words, so let's make some noise!

Prayer:

Aight, Coach of the Cosmos, You've been prepping me for the big leagues of faith. I'm ready to hit the field and put these beliefs into play. Give me the strength to act on what I rep and help me live out loud. No more bench-warming; I'm in the game now. Let's go!

Action:

Think of one way you can put your faith into action today. Maybe it's helping a neighbor, volunteering some time for a good cause, or standing up for what's right when it's easier to just scroll past. Do that thing and watch your faith flex.

Wrap-up your week with a reflection sesh. Look back on your actions and peep the growth. Keep this faith fire kindled, and remember, the squad's stronger with you in it. Stay blessed, keep it righteous, and let's keep this divine connection on the daily. Peace out! 🙏✨

week 4

Day 1

God's Gotchu

Verse of the Day: Jeremiah 29:11 - "For I know the plans I have for you," declares the LORD, "plans to prosper you and not to harm you, plans to give you hope and a future."

Devotional:

Aye, fam, let's get this spiritual party started. Remember, the universe isn't just throwing random levels at you. The Almighty's got a master plan, and it's all about leveling up your game. So when life's getting all kinds of cray, remember God's gotchu.

Prayer:

What's good, Big G? It's your kid here, just trying to navigate this wild ride called life. Sometimes it feels like I'm on the struggle bus with no map. But I trust You got my back. Help me catch those good vibes and spot the signs You're dropping all around me. Bet.

Action:

Today, jot down three things that got you stressed. Flip the script and write down a hope or a positive twist next to each one. Trust the process, and watch God turn those messes into messages.

Day 2

Squad Goals

Verse of the Day: Ecclesiastes 4:9-10 - "Two are better than one, because they have a good return for their labor: If either of them falls down, one can help the other up."

Devotional:

Life ain't a solo mission. It's all about squad goals. Link up with your crew and keep each other on point. Whether you're crushing goals or facing L's, two heads (and hearts) are better than one.

Prayer:

Yo, Creator of the Crew, bless my squad. Help us to have each other's backs like You have ours. Whether we're hyping each other up or picking each other up, let our bond be tighter than that Wi-Fi connection. Amen.

Action:

Hit up your main peeps today. Share something you're working on and ask 'em to keep you accountable. Offer to do the same. Keep that circle tight, encourage each other, and watch those squad goals turn into squad wins.

Day 3

Keep It Real

Verse of the Day: Romans 12:2 - "Do not conform to the pattern of this world, but be transformed by the renewing of your mind."

Devotional:

This world's always trying to play dress-up with your soul, slapping on layers that ain't you. Peel back the fakes and keep it 100. Be the original masterpiece God crafted you to be.

Prayer:

Ayy, Divine Designer, help me to ditch the knock-off vibes and keep it real. Refresh my mind daily so I can rep Your work like the latest drop. No cap.

Action:

Today, catch yourself when you're just going with the flow to fit in. Pause. Reflect on what makes you, YOU. Do one thing that's true to your own style, your own beliefs. Be the trendsetter, not the trend follower.

Day 4

"Good Vibes Only"

Verse of the Day: 1 Thessalonians 5:16-18 - "Rejoice always, pray continually, give thanks in all circumstances; for this is God's will for you in Christ Jesus."

Devotional:

Keep that energy high and that gratitude higher. Life's gonna throw some shade, but you're here to shine bright. Turn up the good vibes with a thankful heart and watch the gloom dip out.

Prayer:

Lord of the Light, hit me with that joy, even when the clouds roll in. I'm 'bout to make thankfulness my jam, and keep the good vibes on blast. Let's get it.

Action:

Create a gratitude list on your phone today. Every time something gets you down, add something you're thankful for. By sunset, you'll have a playlist of blessings that's straight fire.

Day 5

Speak Life

Verse of the Day: Proverbs 18:21 - "The tongue has the power of life and death, and those who love it will eat its fruit."

Devotional:

Your words aren't just tweets or texts—they're life-giving hashtags or hurtful subtweets. Choose to speak life, dropping comments that boost, not roast.

Prayer:

Hey, Word Wizard, guide my tongue today. Let my chats and snaps be all about that life. Help me hype up my friends, my fam, and even that random person who just needs a kind word.

Action:

Today, make it your mission to compliment or encourage at least five people. Slide into their DMs with some positivity or drop a comment that makes them feel seen. Speak life, watch it spread like the

Day 6

Squad Goals

Verse of the Day: Ecclesiastes 4:9-10 - "Two are better than one, because they have a good return for their labor: If either of them falls down, one can help the other up."

Devotional:

Let's get it. Today's about those squad goals—your tribe, your people, your day ones. Faith isn't a solo mission; it's a group chat where everyone's hyping each other up. Look around at your squad. Are they pushing you to level up? Are you doing the same?

Prayer:

Yo, Big G, bless the crew I roll with. Guide us to build each other up, keep each other on track, and not just chase clout but chase Your purpose for us. When one of us takes an L, give us the strength to pick them right back up. Squad goals on point.

Action:

Yo squad, let's roll deep and fuel those dreams. Daily deeds keep us tight—snap your goals, share that progress, and throw high-key hype each other's way. Stay connected, stay motivated, stay slaying. Squad's the power-up we all need. #SquadGoals 🚀👟💥

Day 7

Keep it 100 by Giving Back

Verse of the day: Acts 20:35 - "In everything I did, I showed you that by this kind of hard work we must help the weak, remembering the words the Lord Jesus himself said: 'It is more blessed to give than to receive.'"

Devotional:

Aight, fam, time to flex that giving muscle. It's easy to be all about that get, get, get, but the real key? It's in the give. Find ways to bless others today. Make someone's day, support a cause, or just pass on that positivity.

Prayer:

Lord, You're all about that generosity life. Help me to drop some of that love and kindness on the world today. Keep me focused on the real riches—those good vibes I get from giving back. Let's make this giving thing a whole trend.

Printed in Great Britain
by Amazon

42078537R00040